# VINTAGE GLORY

# VINTAGE GLORY

## Airline Colour Schemes of the '50s and '60s

## Adrian M. Balch

**Airlife**
England

## ACKNOWLEDGEMENTS

Credit for photographs is given where known, but where some photographs have passed through several collections over the years, please forgive me if due credit is not given to the original photographer. I would like to give special thanks to long-standing correspondents Barney Deatrick, Werner Gysin-Aegerter and Stephen Wolf, who have religiously photographed airliners all over the world for at least a quarter-of-a-century. Also, thanks go to John Mounce of Air New Zealand, the Public Relations staff of Lufthansa, United Airlines, to Tom Cole of the Boeing Commercial Airplane Co. and to Brian Stainer of Aviation Photo News.

Credit should also be given to John Roach and Tony Eastwood who produced the following titles, from which most of the individual aircraft histories were obtained:

*Piston Engine Airliner Production List*
*Turbo Prop Airliner Production List*
*Jet Airliner Production List*

These invaluable 'bibles' are currently available from The Aviation Hobby Shop, West Drayton, Middlesex.

I hope you enjoy this nostalgia trip around the world, or wonder at the sights and scenes you have missed.

Adrian M. Balch
June 1994

First published in the UK in 1994
by Airlife Publishing Ltd.

**British Library Cataloguing in Publication Data**
   A catalogue record of this book
   is available from the British Library

ISBN 1 85310 436 1

Printed in Singapore.

# Airlife Publishing Ltd.

101 Longden Road, Shrewsbury SY3 9EB, England

## Front cover

(Top): Loaded with passengers on a charter flight, Aeromaritime Douglas DC-6B, F-BGOB (c/n 43833) claws its way into the air at Bournemouth-Hurn Airport on 3 July 1968. This aircraft served with Aeromaritime/Union de Transports Aeriens since 1964, being withdrawn from use at Le Bourget, Paris, in 1970 and broken up. *(Photo: Stephen Wolf)*

(Bottom left): Capital Airlines Vickers V.745D Viscount, N7443 (c/n 199) over Washington DC in 1957. This aircraft was delivered to Capital on 5 October 1956 and passed on to United Airlines when they merged on 1 June 1961. The aircraft was withdrawn from use in February 1968 and broken up at Burbank, California. *(Photo: Courtesy United Airlines)*

(Bottom right): The scene at Geneva, Switzerland, in 1969 with Vickers V.785 Viscount, I-LIRC (c/n 114) of Alitalia sharing the apron with Sud-Aviation Caravelle III, F-BJTO (c/n 148) of Air France. This Viscount was bought from Capital Airlines in December 1960 and served with Alitalia until being sold to Somali airlines ten years later, in December 1970. *(Photo: via Bernard B. Deatrick)*

## Back cover

(Top left): Many enthusiasts have seen photographs of Short Sandringham, VH-BRC, in the later Ansett Airlines colour scheme with red tail and black/red cheatline. Here it is in its previous colour scheme named "Beachcomber", with light blue cheatline and gold boomerang insignia. Resting between flights at Rose Bay, Sydney, the photograph was taken on 23 May 1964. Who would have thought that thirty years later, this very aircraft would be the centre of attraction inside the Southampton Hall of Aviation. *(Photo: Bernard B. Deatrick)*

(Top right): American Airlines Douglas DC-6B, N90763 (c/n 43546) "Flagship Nashville" awaits its next load of passengers at an unknown Stateside location in 1965. It was delivered new to the airline in October 1951. It gave faithful service until being sold in March 1966. It was withdrawn from use in 1980 and broken up. *(Photo: Author's collection)*

(Bottom left): A unique sight at airports throughout Europe during the 1950s and '60s was the Breguet 763 Provence, of which Air France operated twelve including F-BASX (c/n 10) shown here at Paris-Orly in April 1969. In 1965, six of these aircraft were converted to Universal freighters, including this one, giving it a joint freight/passenger role with about 30 passengers in the upper deck and freight in the lower. This example was retired in July 1971 and delivered to the Aero Club Air France at Toussus-le-Noble for preservation, but had to be scrapped by 1979. *(Photo: Dr Jean-M. Magendie)*

(Bottom right): It's a good job there wasn't a double-decker bus coming along the main A38 Bristol to Bridgwater road when this SPANTAX Douglas DC-7C came in to land at Bristol-Lulsgate Airport in June 1967! Bought from Alitalia in April 1966, EC-BDL (c/n 45230) was one of five DC-7s operated on holiday charter flights throughout Europe until it was withdrawn from use in 1979 and used as a restaurant near Las Palomas, Gran Canaria, Tenerife. *(Photo: via Stephen Wolf)*

## Half title page

BEA operated eight examples of the Armstrong-Whitworth Argosy on freight and general cargo duties during the '60s. Here, Argosy 222, G-ASXM (c/n 6801) is seen on finals to Heathrow on 26 April 1968. This aircraft was delivered to BEA in March 1965 and was sold to Transair in Canada in June 1970. Its last operator was SAFE Air in New Zealand who withdrew it from use, when the airline ceased operations, in early 1991. *(Photo: Stephen Wolf)*

## Title page

One of the most photogenic airports must be Geneva, Switzerland, in winter where we see Swissair Sud-Aviation SE-210 Caravelle III, HB-ICU (c/n 123) in this perfect Christmas card setting in January 1965. HB-ICU was one of nine Caravelles operated by Swissair from 1962 to 1970. This aircraft was still flying with a small airline in Zaire in 1992. *(Photo: Werner Gysin-Aegerter)*

# INTRODUCTION

This is the third in Airlife's 'Glory' series; *Faded Glory* covers airliners in the '70s, *Flying Colours* covers the '80s and now *Vintage Glory* covers the missing era that is possible to cover all in colour – the '50s and '60s.

Readers will probably come in two categories, those of my generation who will revel in a nostalgia trip from their schoolboy spotting days. The second category will be those of a younger generation, who can marvel at the propliners and first jetliners in early colour schemes around the world. The '50s and '60s were a paradise for aircraft spotters and photographers. SLR cameras and telephoto lenses were in their infancy,

yet were not necessary to obtain good photographs, as there was not the terrorist threat that exists today, no high fences, no thick glass through which to view airliners and generally less hassle and tension in the world. You could stand on the roof gardens and public viewing areas at London's Heathrow and Gatwick airports, for example, and take full-frame photographs of airliners taxiing in and parking with a fixed standard-lens camera . . . often they were too close! The variety of sights and sounds was wonderful, when every other aircraft wasn't an Airbus, a Jumbo or a 737.

I started taking colour slides in 1966, just in time to capture the end of the

piston propliner era, but many of the photographs in this book are taken by enthusiasts of a previous generation, some of whom are regretfully deceased. It is mainly due to them that this book is possible, produced from colour slides when Kodak first started producing colour slide film called *Kodachrome 1*, followed by *Kodachrome II*, which were the predecessors of today's *Kodachrome 25* film.

The one criteria, when selecting photographs for this book, is that they were all taken in the 1950s or '60s. Anything taken later than 1969 was rejected.

# PHOTOGRAPH INDEX

(Right)
Vickers V.701 Viscount, G-AMOH (c/n 21) of Cambrian Airways on a scheduled service at Bristol-Lulsgate Airport in June 1968. The 700 series Viscount could readily be distinguished from the later 800 series by the cockpit window blind and the oval front passenger door. This aircraft was previously with Channel Airways until April 1965. Cambrian were the final operator, the aircraft being withdrawn from use in November 1971. It was broken up at Cardiff in September 1972. *(Photo: Dave Cross)*

(Below)
Bristol 170 Freighter Mk.31, G-APLH (c/n 13250), of Dan-Air Services Ltd at London-Gatwick Airport on 19 June 1965. It was delivered new on 31 March 1958 and served on general cargo duties until it was sold to Thomas Lamb Airways of Canada in November 1968. *(Photo: Clive Moggridge)*

Douglas DC-3, G-ALXL (c/n 33235) of Cambrian Airways at its home base of Cardiff-Rhoose in August 1963, awaiting its next load of passengers. This aircraft was bought from BEA in April 1962 and sold in April 1969. It was broken up in Bahrain in April 1976. *(Photo: H. J. Balch)*

Airspeed AS.57 Ambassador, G-AMAH (c/n 5230), of Dan-Air Services Ltd caught with its two Bristol Centaurus engines spluttering into life at Paris-Le Bourget in June 1968. This was the last of 23 Ambassadors to be built, serving with Dan-Air from November 1959 until being withdrawn from use in November 1971 and scrapped. Dan-Air ceased operations on 23 October 1992.

*(Photo: Dr Jean-M. Magendie)*

(Right)
On a typical British overcast day, BAC One-Eleven 408EF, G-AVGP (c/n 114) of Autair International is seen during a test flight from the BAC factory at Bournemouth-Hurn on 16 January 1969. After a change of name to Court Line, it was sold to Cambrian Airways in April 1970, which was absorbed into British Airways in April 1976. G-AVGP was withdrawn from use in November 1988.
*(Photo: Stephen Wolf)*

(Below)
Airspeed AS.57 Ambassador, G-ALZS (c/n 5215) of Autair International at Lourdes in 1967. Autair bought this aircraft from Globe Air in November 1963. Shortly after this photograph was taken, G-ALZS was damaged beyond repair after aquaplaning at Luton, Bedfordshire, on 14 September 1967. On 1 January 1970 Autair changed its name to Court Line until 15 August 1974, when they ceased operations.
*(Photo: Dr Jean-M. Magendie)*

(Above)
Eagle Airways changed its name to Cunard Eagle Airways on 5 January 1961, when the Cunard Steamship Company took over 60 per cent of the company's interests. Bristol Britannia 324, G-ARKA (c/n 13516) is seen here at Heathrow Airport in 1962. In October 1963 the airline changed its name to British Eagle International Airlines. G-ARKA was leased to Tellair of Switzerland from 24 March 1969, until it was withdrawn from use in November 1969 and scrapped at Coventry in October 1971. *(Photo: Brian Stainer/APN)*

(Right)
Seen a long way from home is Douglas DC-6A, G-ARMY (c/n 45457) of British Eagle International Airlines at Adelaide, Australia, on 11 November 1963. This aircraft was with Overseas National Airways until March 1961, when it was bought by Cunard Eagle Airways who changed its name to British Eagle in October 1963. G-ARMY was sold to Saudi Arabian Airlines in March 1964, who donated it to Yemen Airways in 1971, shortly after which it was withdrawn from use and scrapped. *(Photo: via Barney Deatrick)*

Preparing to take-off from London-Heathrow Airport in September 1968 is Bristol Britannia 311, G-AOVA (c/n 13217) of British Eagle International Airlines. The airline operated this aircraft from April 1964 until 6 November 1968, when the airline ceased operations. This aircraft then went to Caledonian Airways, followed by Lloyd International, before finally being scrapped at Coventry in October 1971. *(Photo: Bob Griggs)*

Pan-Am in its heyday. Douglas DC-6B, N6110C (c/n 44110) seen at Frankfurt on 10 May 1963 with tails of a Boeing 707 and DC-8 behind. This aircraft was withdrawn from use in March 1968, but went on to serve with smaller airlines until final withdrawal from service in December 1979. It was broken up at Fort Lauderdale, Florida, in 1983. *(Photo: Author's collection)*

(Above)
Operating from Manston, Kent, Invicta Airways bought Vickers V.755 Viscount, G-AOCB (c/n 92) from British Eagle in November 1967, until Invicta merged with British Midland Airways in March 1969. G-AOCB is seen here at Birmingham-Elmdon on 12 June 1968. *(Photo: Bob Griggs)*

(Left)
Overseas Aviation Ltd was formed in 1957 and bought Canadair C-4 Argonaut, G-ALHU (c/n 166) from BOAC on 30 January 1959 which saw service only until April 1960. The Argonaut was a Canadair-built Douglas DC-4 with Rolls-Royce Merlin Engines of which Overseas Aviation operated nine during 1959-60. The airline was short-lived, ceasing operations in August 1961. Argonaut, G-ALHU, is seen here at Cambridge in January 1960. It was sold to Flying Enterprise of Denmark, with whom it ended its days, being broken up at Kastrup, Copenhagen in July 1965.
*(Photo: Bob Griggs)*

A really vintage scene at Heathrow in 1957, with Airspeed Ambassador, G-ALZT (c/n 5216), of British European Airways being prepared for departure, while Convair CV-340, I-DOGU, of Alitalia taxies past. In the background can be seen a Viscount and DC-3 of BEA. The Ambassador served with BEA from January 1952 until May 1958, when it was sold to BKS Air Transport. It was withdrawn from use by BKS at Newcastle in October 1967 and scrapped the following year. *(Photo: Bob Griggs)*

(Above)
A sight rarely seen these days – an airline colour scheme employing polished natural metal. Vickers V.701 Viscount, G-AMOB (c/n 11) is seen at Cambridge in 1959, resplendent in its original BEA colour scheme and named RMA *William Baffin*. BEA took delivery of this aircraft on 24 April 1955 and it served until being sold to VASP of Brazil in August 1962. It was withdrawn from use in April 1970 and broken up at Rio in July 1979.
*(Photo: Bob Griggs)*

(Right)
BEA changed their colour scheme in 1959 to that shown here on Vickers V.806 Viscount, G-AOYR (c/n 266) at Gatwick in May 1968. This particular Viscount served with BEA from April 1958 until being sold to BKS Air Transport in December 1969. In 1992, it was still flying, serving with British Air Ferries at Southend, looking as pristine as the day it was delivered to BEA.
*(Photo: Bob Griggs)*

(Above)
The last aircraft to be delivered to BEA in the 'red square' colour scheme was the BAC One-Eleven 510 series. Here, G-AVMJ (c/n 138) is depicted outside the BAC factory at Bournemouth-Hurn in August 1968, prior to delivery. It was finally delivered a year later, on 29 August 1969, and remained with BEA throughout the merger with BOAC in April 1974, finally being withdrawn from use by the resulting British Airways in 1992. *(Photo: Adrian Balch)*

(Right)
A classic scene from the roof gardens at Heathrow Airport in 1962 with BEA Vanguard, G-APEN, surrounded by BEA and BOAC ground equipment and vehicles. In the background can be seen a Caravelle of Scandinavian Airlines System and a Viscount of BEA.
*(Photo: Author's collection)*

You can almost hear the four Rolls-Royce Tyne turboprops whining, as this BEA Vickers Vanguard taxies in at Heathrow in May 1964. G-APED (c/n 707) was one of twenty Vanguards operated by British European Airways and entered service on 30 January 1961. It remained with BEA all its life, being withdrawn from use and broken up at Heathrow in May 1973.
*(Photo: Bob Griggs)*

(Right)
In 1968, British European Airways changed their colour scheme again to that shown here on Vickers V.802 Viscount, G-AOJD (c/n 153) in July 1969. Another Viscount is seen in the old scheme behind.
*(Photo: Bob Griggs)*

(Below)
The last British operator of the Canadair C-4 Argonaut was British Midland Airways, whose G-ALHS (c/n 164) is seen here about to depart East Midlands Airport in 1967. This particular aircraft was bought from Overseas Aviation in February 1960, by Derby Airways, who changed their name to British Midland Airways on 1 October 1964. 'HS was withdrawn from use in October 1967 and broken up in 1970.
*(Photo: Courtesy The Aviation Hobby Shop)*

Throughout the 1950s and early '60s, the scene at Hurn Airport, Bournemouth, was dominated by the Bristol Freighter on car and passenger-carrying flights to France and Belgium. Here, Bristol 170 Mk.32 Superfreighter, G-AMWE (c/n 13132) of British United Air Ferries is seen taxying out at Hurn in September 1965 bound for the Continent. This aircraft was delivered to Silver City Airways in March 1956, who changed their name to British United Air Ferries on 1 June 1963. 'WE was withdrawn from use in December 1965 and broken up at Lydd, Kent, in 1967. *(Photo: Werner Gysin-Aegerter)*

Aviation Traders Ltd of Southend produced a successful conversion of the Douglas DC-4 in the '60s to carry cars, replacing the Bristol Freighters. Known as the Carvair (car-via-air), twenty-one conversions were produced of which G-ASKN (c/n 13/3058) of British United Air Ferries is seen at Southend in 1966. This aircraft was delivered to BUAF in February 1964 and went on to serve with British Air Ferries until it was sold in June 1976 to a construction company in the Congo. It was withdrawn from use there in 1978. *(Photo: Clive Moggridge)*

(Left)
Bristol 170 Mk.32 Superfreighter, G-ANWK (c/n 13259) of British Air Ferries at the Biggin Hill Air Fair in May 1968. On 1 October 1967, British United Air Ferries changed their name to British Air Ferries and this was the final colour scheme for this aircraft, which was withdrawn from use in October 1969 and broken up at Lydd the following year.
*(Photo: Clive Moggridge)*

(Below)
Douglas DC-6A, G-APNP (c/n 45532) of Air Ferry on a rain-soaked apron at Gatwick Airport on 15 August 1968. This aircraft was transferred from British United Airways to Air Ferry Ltd in July 1965 and was sold to Balair of Switzerland in January 1969. It was ill-fated, however, for when operating on lease to the International Red Cross, it crashed in Biafra on 7 May 1969. *(Photo: Stephen Wolf)*

Another wet day at Gatwick Airport on 17 May 1969 with passengers boarding a British United Airways Viscount, behind which stands Vickers V.833 Viscount, G-APTC (c/n 425) resplendent in BUA's second colour scheme. This aircraft was sold to Arkia-Israel Inland Airlines in October 1969, but crashed at Tel Aviv on 26 October 1969 on a night training flight. *(Photo: Stephen Wolf)*

(Left)
The orange dayglo nose and tail on Douglas DC-3, G-AOBN, identifies this as a British United Airways Calibration Unit aircraft, when seen at Gatwick in 1965. This aircraft last served with Ethiopian Airlines until 12 August 1977 when it was destroyed on the ground at Jiggiga Airfield.
*(Photo: Clive Moggridge)*

(Below)
Air France Douglas DC-3s were a familiar sight at Paris's Le Bourget and Orly airports during the '50s and '60s, mainly used for freight and postal services. Here, F-BEFN (c/n 12892) sits at Orly on 6 June 1969 ready for the night postal flight. Air France bought this aircraft from the USAF after the war in July 1947 and it was sold in the USA in September 1969. It was last known derelict in Barbados by November 1978 and has probably expired by now.
*(Photo: Author's collection)*

Seen in its original British United Airways colour scheme is BAC One-Eleven 210AC, G-ASJF (c/n 10) disembarking another load of passengers at Gatwick in July 1966. This aircraft was delivered to BUA in July 1965 and was sold to Pacific Express of Florida in April 1982, when BUA merged with Caledonian Airways to form British Caledonian. The aircraft last flew with Florida Express until February 1986, when it was withdrawn from use and broken up.
*(Photo: Peter Middlebrook)*

(Above) In 1967, BUA changed its colour scheme to that shown on BAC One-Eleven 210AC, G-ASJE (c/n 9) on a sunny day at Gatwick in September 1969. It also ended its days being broken up at Orlando, Florida, in 1990. *(Photo: Bob Griggs)*

(Left) The Handley Page Herald's sales suffered at the hands of its rival, the Fokker Friendship. Initially, the Herald was built with four Alvis Leonides piston engines, but orders soon came in when the engines were changed to two Rolls-Royce Dart turboprops, although only 50 were built. This made the Herald a rarity for spotters and photographers alike. Here, Handley Page Herald 213, D-BEBE (c/n 179) of Bavaria Fluggesellschaft taxies out at Hannover on 3 May 1968. This aircraft entered service in March 1965 and was sold to Arkia in November 1968. It last served with Channel Express at Bournemouth, registered G-AYMG and was withdrawn from use in 1993 being reduced to spares. *(Photo: Author's collection)*

(Right)
A rare photograph of British Overseas Airways Corporation Bristol Britannia 312, G-AOVD (c/n 13235) at Cambridge in 1958. This aircraft was delivered to BOAC on 6 December 1957, but crashed in fog near Christchurch, Dorset, on Christmas Eve 1958. (Photo: Bob Griggs)

(Below)
Canadair licence-built the Britannia in Canada, incorporating a swing-tail cargo door and re-engining it with Rolls-Royce Tyne turboprops. Designated Canadair CL-44, thirty-nine were built for civil and military use. Here, CL-44D4, G-AWDK (c/n 23) of Transglobe Airways is seen taxying at Gatwick on 15 August 1968. Transglobe leased this aircraft from Seaboard World Airlines from April to August 1968, making this photograph fairly rare. This aircraft ended its days with Bayu Indonesia and was withdrawn from use at Jakarta in 1990. (Photo: Stephen Wolf)

One of the smartest liveries applied to the Britannia was that of Treffield International, whose Britannia 102, G-ANBM (c/n 12914) is seen on a wet day at Gatwick in May 1967. Treffield leased this Britannia from Laker Airways for only one month from May to June 1967, before operations ceased. 'BM ended its days being broken up at Jakarta, Indonesia, in December 1971, following its sale to Ankasa Civil Air Transport in February 1969. *(Photo: Author's collection)*

(Above)
Douglas C-54A Skymaster, G-ARLF (c/n 10278) of Lloyd International Airways in 1961 at Cambridge, before flying to Malaga, Spain where it was destroyed by fire whilst refuelling on 8 October 1961. Photographs of 'RLF in this livery are rare, as it was in service with Lloyd for only seven months, having been bought from Icelandic airline, Loftleidir on 11 March 1961. *(Photo: Bob Griggs)*

(Right)
Douglas DC-6B, CF-CUQ (c/n 43844) was delivered new to Canadian Pacific Airlines on 26 February 1953. Named "Empress of City of Buenos Aires", it is seen in its final livery taxiing at Sea Island, Vancouver, on 5 April 1964. The following year, it crashed after a bomb explosion at Dog Creek, 330 kilometres north of Vancouver, British Columbia, on 8 July 1965.
*(Photo: Bernard B. Deatrick)*

The pride of BOAC during the late '50s and early '60s was the de Havilland Comet 4 which pioneered jet trans-Atlantic air travel. Here, Comet 4, G-APDD (c/n 6405) is seen taxying in at Heathrow in May 1964. It was delivered to BOAC on 18 November 1958 and sold to Malaysian Airways on 8 November 1965. It last served with Dan-Air, being broken up at Lasham in March 1973. *(Photo: Bob Griggs)*

(Above)
A line-up of BOAC Bristol Britannias Series 102, at Cambridge in June 1964 after withdrawal from service, awaiting sale. G-ANBM (c/n 12914), nearest, went out on lease to Laker Airways on 8 April 1966 and was leased to Treffield International for a month the following year.
*(Photo: Bob Griggs)*

(Right)
A familiar sight around European airports was this cargo-configured Douglas DC-4 Skymaster, G-APEZ (c/n 42921) which spent much of its time on Government cargo flights operating out of RAF Lyneham, alongside the airline's L-749 Constellations. G-APEZ was bought from Starways in 1964 and withdrawn from use at Coventry in July 1966, being scrapped there two years later. It is seen at the Biggin Hill Air Fair in May 1965.
*(Photo: Peter Middlebrook)*

Showing an obviously overpainted BEA cheatline, Vickers Viking G-AMNR (c/n 291) is seen in Continental Air Transport livery at Rotterdam in 1960. This small airline's fleet included four Vikings, during its short life from November 1957 until operations ceased in October 1960.
*(Photo: Author's collection)*

(Right)
Ill-fated de Havilland Comet 4C, OD-ADQ (c/n 6446) of Middle East Airlines being towed along the taxiway at Heathrow in 1967. This aircraft was delivered to the airline on 15 February 1961 and destroyed in an Israeli commando attack at Beirut, Lebanon, on 28 December 1968.
*(Photo: Bob Griggs)*

(Below)
Rare shot of BOAC Comet 4, G-APDP (c/n 6417) while leased to Air Ceylon (now Sri Lanka), seen parked in BOAC's maintenance area at Heathrow in May 1964. This aircraft ended its days as XX944 with the Royal Aircraft Establishment at Farnborough, who bought the aircraft from Dan-Air in March 1973 and withdrew it from use at Farnborough in April 1975, where it was scrapped.
*(Photo: Bob Griggs)*

Vickers V.708 Viscount, F-BGNN (c/n 14) was delivered new to Air France in October 1953 until it was sold to Maitland Drewery Aviation in December 1960. The aircraft ended its days with MMM Aero Services of Zaire, being broken up at Kinshasa in January 1987. The aircraft is seen at Heathrow in 1957, while operating a Paris shuttle. *(Photo: Bob Griggs)*

A classic scene at Heathrow Airport in November 1966, with Icelandair Douglas DC-6B, TF-FIP (c/n 43549) in the foreground. Named "Solfaxi", this aircraft was bought from Scandinavian Airlines System in January 1964 and was sold to Belgian airline, Delta Air Transport in April 1972. This is one of the few DC-6s still airworthy and is currently operated as a firebomber by Conifair in Canada. It is interesting to note that all the aircraft in this photograph are propliners, apart from a BOAC VC-10 and a BEA Comet 4B. See how many you can identify in the background? *(Photo: Bob Griggs)*

(Left)
Another view from the Queen's Building at Heathrow Airport in 1961, showing Douglas DC-7C, EP-AEP (c/n 45158) of Persian Air Services, which was OO-SFB leased from SABENA from 13 May 1961 to 18 January 1962. This aircraft is one of the few remaining airworthy DC-7s at the time of writing, last being used for cargo work by T. & G. Aviation out of Miami.
*(Photo: Brian Stainer/APN)*

(Below)
Throughout the '60s, the Tupolev TU-104 was about the only Aeroflot-type seen at Heathrow and that was only about once a week. Rare appearances were made by the odd Ilyushin IL-18 or Antonov AN-12, but the TU-104 made a unique sight with those operated by Aeroflot being quite rare and those operated by CSA-Czechoslovakian Airlines even rarer. Here, CCCP-42403 is seen being manoeuvred by a BEA ground handling crew in this 1969 view.
*(Photo: Author's collection)*

(Above)
"Queen of the Skies" Lockheed L-1049H Super Constellation, AP-AJZ (c/n 4836) of Pakistan International Airlines sits outside BOAC's maintenance base at Heathrow in 1966. This aircraft served all its life with PIA, being delivered on 3 March 1958. It was withdrawn from use in 1969 and donated to the Indonesian Air Force, but is not thought to have flown in their markings. Its current status is unknown. (Photo: Dr Jean-M. Magendie)

(Right)
For years, the only Lockheed Electras seen in Europe were those operated by KLM-Royal Dutch Airlines. Here, PH-LLC (c/n 2006) named "Mars", is seen arriving at Heathrow in 1962. It was one of twelve bought by KLM in 1959 and sold to Universal Airlines in November 1968. It is currently in service with Falcon Cargo of Sweden, registered SE-IVR, who bought it in October 1986. (Photo: Author's collection)

An excellent view of Sud-Aviation SE-210 Caravelle OO-SRF (c/n 76) of SABENA-Belgian World Airlines at Brussels in 1966. It was one of ten bought new by SABENA in 1961. Although it was leased to several airlines during its life, it was finally sold to Europe Air Service in 1978, who flew it for another ten years, withdrawing it from use in February 1988.
*(Photo: via Bernard B. Deatrick)*

(Right) Aer Lingus was the first airline to buy the Fokker F.27 Friendship, operating seven, of which EI-AKG (c/n 10119) is seen taxying at Heathrow in 1964. Named "Fiachra", this particular example was delivered on 12 May 1959 and was sold back to Fokker in March 1966. It was last known in service with SASCO of Sudan, registered ST-EVF since April 1986. (Photo: Brian Stainer/APN)

(Below) At times, the aircraft at Gatwick Airport were parked too close to the public viewing area (in the foreground) for a standard-lens photograph. The only answer was to move to a viewing area further away and use a telephoto lens! This Luxair Lockheed L-1649A Starliner, LX-LGY (c/n 1036) was one of three that used to park in this manner at Gatwick and was captured there on 15 August 1968, shortly before all those wonderful public viewing piers were closed and the public moved a long way away on top of the current terminal. LX-LGY was leased from Trek Airways from April 1966 until October 1968. It was last operated by Nittler Air Transport, who abandoned it at Doula, Cameroons, in 1971 and by 1980, it had been broken up. (Photo: Stephen Wolf)

A rare type anywhere was the Convair 880, as only 65 were built. Cathay Pacific Airways operated nine during the '60s, of which VR-HFX was bought from VIASA of Venezuela in November 1965, but crashed at Hong Kong on 5 November 1967. It is seen here at Hong Kong during May 1967 in between domestic flights. Note the shaded stairs to offer some protection from the scorching Far East summer sun.
*(Photo: Peter R. Keating)*

The Handley Page Herald faced fierce competition from the Fokker Friendship, making the former a rarity at airports around the world. Globe Air operated five Heralds including Srs.210, HB-AAK (c/n 1743) named "Herald of Basle" from March 1964 until July 1968, when it was sold to Europe Aero Service. It is seen at Basel, Switzerland, in May 1968. This aircraft is still in service with Channel Express Air Services, who registered it G-SCTT in August 1988.
*(Photo: Werner Gysin-Aegerter)*

(Above)
Operating charter flights from France to the UK Douglas DC-6B, F-BNUZ (c/n 45173) of Trans-Union was a regular visitor to London-Gatwick and was caught there on a very wet 17 May 1969. It was bought from Japan Air Lines in September 1966 and damaged beyond repair after a heavy landing at Nice, France on 22 October 1971, just after being transferred to Europe Aero Service. It was broken up two months later. (Photo: Stephen Wolf)

(Left)
The most common operator of the Ilyushin IL-18 into London-Heathrow throughout the '60s was LOT-Polish Airlines, which has operated nine of the type for over thirty years, including SP-LSB seen taxying in at Heathrow in May 1964.
(Photo: Bob Griggs)

(Above)
A common type in rare markings is this Douglas DC-6B, YK-AEC (c/n 44170) of Syrian Arab Airlines seen taxying at Paris-Le Bourget Airport in September 1965. This aircraft was transferred from Unit Arab Airlines in February 1961 and withdrawn from use at Damascus in 1974.

*(Photo: Werner Gysin-Aegerter)*

(Right)
Across the other side of the world at Manila Airport, Philippines, Douglas DC-4 Skymaster, PI-C775 (c/n 10296), of Philippine Air Lines taxies in after a domestic flight. This aircraft was bought from Japan Air Lines in June 1964 and sold in the USA in November 1968.

*(Photo: Bernard B. Deatrick)*

Only 23 Airspeed Ambassadors were built, of which G-ALZR (c/n 5214) is shown here in BKS Air Transport's second and final livery at Heathrow in 1965. This aircraft was bought from Rolls-Royce in May 1963 and converted to a freighter in November 1964. It was damaged beyond repair at Gatwick on 26 July 1969 and bought by Dan-Air for spares in November 1969, when it was broken up at Lasham.
*(Photo: Author's collection)*

Although Aerolineas Argentinas operated six Comet 4 variants during the '50s and '60s, LV-AIB was their sole Mark 4C with longer nose and extended range. It was delivered in April 1962 and sold to Dan-Air in October 1971. It was withdrawn from use in November 1977 and broken up the following year at Lasham. LV-AIB is seen here at Heathrow in January 1967, preparing to depart for Buenos Aires. *(Photo: Brian Stainer)*

A wonderfully nostalgic scene at Bangkok, Thailand, in September 1962 with Lufthansa Boeing 707-430, D-ABOG (c/n 18056) surrounded by a BOAC Bristol Britannia in the foreground, Air India Boeing 707-437 to the left and Pan-American Douglas DC-8-32, N815PA, taxying behind. This Lufthansa Boeing 707 is seen in its original livery and was delivered new to the airline the previous year. It was sold in October 1976 and last heard of in store at Tel Aviv, Israel, having been bought by Israeli Aircraft Industries in March 1982.
*(Photo: Bernard B. Deatrick)*

(Above)
At Kai Tak Airport, Hong Kong, de Havilland Comet 4, 9V-BAT (c/n 6404) of Malaysia-Singapore Airlines is seen taxying out on 18 March 1969. This aircraft was previously G-APDC with BOAC until bought by the airline in October 1965. It was sold to Dan-Air in August 1969 and withdrawn from use in April 1973, being broken up at Lasham two years later. *(Photo: Bernard B. Deatrick)*

(Right)
An unusually peaceful scene at Beirut, Lebanon, with Vickers V.754D Viscount, OD-ACV (c/n 241) of Middle East Airlines awaiting another load of passengers for a domestic flight. This aircraft was sold to Central African Airways in February 1961 and last known withdrawn from use in August 1984 at Harare, Zimbabwe, after service with Air Zimbabwe.

*(Photo: Author's collection)*

(Right)
Just how exotic can you get? A Curtiss C-46A Commando, XW-PCU, of Royal Air Lao prepares to depart Kai Tak Airport, Hong Kong, on 4 March 1966, no doubt bound for Vientiane.
*(Photo: Bernard B. Deatrick)*

(Below)
Bristol Britannia 318, OK-MBB (c/n 13515) was CU-T671 of CUBANA leased by CSA-Ceskoslovenske Aerolinie from March 1963 to January 1969. Apart from this lease, it has served all its life with CUBANA, from delivery in August 1959 to withdrawal and scrapping at Havana in 1990. This aircraft is seen at Cambridge in 1964, during routine servicing by Marshalls. *(Photo: Bob Griggs)*

(Above)
The Flying Dutchman – KLM Lockheed L-1049G Super Constellation, PH-LKK (c/n 4645) named "Centaurus" seen taxying at Idlewild Airport, New York, in May 1958, with a Lufthansa Super Constellation and Alitalia Douglas DC-7C in the background. PH-LKK was delivered new to KLM in June 1956 and sold to Iberia in August 1962. Its final days were employed in Biafra relief flights, when it crashed on approach to Port Harcourt, Biafra, in January 1968.
*(Photo: via Dr Jean-M. Magendie)*

(Right)
Bristol Britannia 312, EC-BFJ (c/n 13429) of Air Spain at Cambridge in April 1967. This aircraft was originally G-AOVR with BOAC and British Eagle, who sold it to Air Spain in October 1966. After many charter flights to Gatwick, it was sold to IAS Cargo Airlines in April 1973, who used it for spares at Biggin Hill. It was broken up in 1974. *(Photo: Bob Griggs)*

Another familiar visitor to Gatwick in the '60s was Douglas DC-7B, SE-ERD (c/n 45089) of Transair Sweden AB, depicted on 15 August 1968. This airline operated many charter flights with this aircraft from March 1965 until October 1969, when it was withdrawn from use and scrapped at Malmo, Sweden.
*(Photo: Stephen Wolf)*

This very rare photograph depicts KLM Lockheed Electra, PH-LLD during its one year lease to Air Ceylon (now Sri Lanka) from 1 November 1960 to 1 November 1961. Viewed from the Queen's Building at London-Heathrow in 1961, this aircraft was last reported in store at Marana, Arizona, in December 1984.
*(Photo: Brian Stainer/APN)*

(Above) The Avro York had the wings and tails of the Lancaster to thank for its classic lines. G-AGNV (c/n 1223) of Skyways of London is depicted in a wintery setting at London-Heathrow in early 1964. It was bought from BOAC in March 1955 and operated by Skyways until May 1964, when it was retired to Luton and stored. On 9 October 1964, it was donated to the Skyfame Museum at Staverton, Gloucestershire, and made its last flight there, where it was painted up as Winston Churchill's 'LV633' 'Ascalon'. It was later transferred to the Cosford Aerospace Museum, where it was repainted in post-war RAF markings as 'MW100'. It is one of only two Yorks extant today, the other being G-ANTK at Duxford. *(Photo: Author's collection)*

(Left) Another classic Heathrow scene in 1960, with Lockheed L-749A Constellation, G-ANUR (c/n 2565) of Skyways of London dominating the picture. This aircraft was leased from BOAC from July 1959 and bought from them three years later. It was transferred to Euravia (who became Britannia Airways) in September 1962 and ended its days being broken up at Montevideo, Uruguay, in 1970.
*(Photo: Author's collection)*

(Right)
The initial batch of fifteen Boeing 707s for British Overseas Airways Corporation were ordered in 1956 and powered by Rolls-Royce Conway engines. The first of these was 707-436, G-APFB (c/n 17703) which is depicted just prior to delivery in May 1960. The 707 entered regular service with BOAC on the London-New York route on 6 June 1960, supplementing Comets and Britannias. G-APFB spent all its life with BOAC and subsequently British Airways until 1976, when it was traded back to Boeing, who scrapped it at Kingman, Arizona, in 1979. *(Photo: Boeing)*

(Below)
Resplendent in its original colour scheme is the first Boeing 707-227, N7071 (c/n 17691) for Braniff International Airways over Washington State in October 1959. Regretfully, this aircraft never got delivered, as it was written off on its acceptance flight on 19 October 1959 at Arlington, Washington. *(Photo: Boeing)*

Braniff International Airways revolutionised airline colour schemes by painting its aircraft in one of seven fuselage colours during the mid-60s. Blue Boeing 707-327C, N7099 (c/n 19108) is seen taxying at Honolulu, Hawaii, on 8 February 1968. It was delivered new to Braniff in July 1966 and sold to Trans Mediterranean Airways of Lebanon in July 1972. It was withdrawn from use and stored at Beirut in 1991.
*(Photo: Bernard B. Deatrick)*

On 1 June 1964, Trans Canada Airlines changed its name to Air Canada and Vickers V.757 Viscount, CF-THR (c/n 278) is seen in the revised livery in August 1969. It was withdrawn from use and stored at Winnipeg in March 1971 and ended its days being broken up in 1975. *(Photo: via Bernard B. Deatrick)*

Braniff International Airways revolutionised airline colour schemes by painting its aircraft in one of seven fuselage colours during the mid-60s. Blue Boeing 707-327C, N7099 (c/n 19108) is seen taxying at Honolulu, Hawaii, on 8 February 1968. It was delivered new to Braniff in July 1966 and sold to Trans Mediterranean Airways of Lebanon in July 1972. It was withdrawn from use and stored at Beirut in 1991.
*(Photo: Bernard B. Deatrick)*

(Above)
A classic colour scheme on a classic airliner – Trans World Airlines Boeing 707-331B, N18709 (c/n 18985) is seen taxying at Paris-Orly in June 1969. This aircraft was sold to El Al of Israel in April 1982 and last used by Boeing in their KC-135E programme, being broken up in 1990. *(Photo: Bob Griggs)*

(Right)
Apart from BEA, the only other airline to order the Vickers Vanguard was Trans Canada Airlines, who had 23.CF-TKT (c/n 743) delivered in October 1961 and repainted in Air Canada livery when the airline changed its name on 1 June 1964. It was sold to Europe Aero Service in November 1972 and withdrawn from use in 1977, being broken up at Perpignan, France, the following year. CF-TKT is seen at Sea Island, Vancouver, on 5 April 1964.
*(Photo: Bernard B. Deatrick)*

Trans Canada Airlines' intercontinental routes were flown by a fleet of 13 DC-8s from 1 June 1960, replacing Super Constellations on the Montreal-London route. The fifth aircraft delivered was DC-8-42, CF-TJE (c/n 45565) which was delivered in November 1960, changed its colours to Air Canada in June 1964 and sold to the FAA in September 1975, with whom it was destroyed in tests in June 1978. *(Photo: Bernard B. Deatrick)*

On 1 June 1964, Trans Canada Airlines changed its name to Air Canada and Vickers V.757 Viscount, CF-THR (c/n 278) is seen in the revised livery in August 1969. It was withdrawn from use and stored at Winnipeg in March 1971 and ended its days being broken up in 1975.
*(Photo: via Bernard B. Deatrick)*

(Left)
Currently merged into Canadian Airlines International, Canadian Pacific Airlines operated a fleet of eight Bristol Britannias during the late '50s-early '60s including Srs.314, CF-CZA (13393) "Empress of Hong Kong" seen at Sea Island, Vancouver on 5 April 1964 in its second Canadian Pacific livery. Delivered new in April 1958, this was sold in May 1965 and was finally broken up at Biggin Hill in December 1971. *(Photo: Bernard B. Deatrick)*

(Below)
Alongside the Britannias, Canadian Pacific Airlines initially operated a fleet of five DC-8s on intercontinental routes including DC-8-43, CF-CPI (c/n 45622) "Empress of Calgary", which was delivered in May 1961 and sold in November 1980 after the airline was renamed CP Air. The aircraft was last reported with the Opa-Locka Fire Dept, Florida, in December 1982, so its fate is assured. It is seen taxying out at Sea Island, Vancouver, on 5 April 1964.
*(Photo: Bernard B. Deatrick)*

Seen at Auckland, New Zealand, is Vickers V.807 Viscount, ZK-BRF (c/n 283) of New Zealand National Airways Corporation being prepared for another local flight on 26 January 1964. This aircraft is named "City of Christchurch" and was one of four delivered new to NZNAC in 1959. It was withdrawn from use in 1975 and is in store for preservation. (Photo: Bernard B. Deatrick)

(Left)
Seen high above New Zealand, Douglas DC-3, ZK-AOD (c/n 27146) of New Zealand National Airways Corporation was one of a large fleet operated from 1947 to 1969. This photograph was probably taken in 1963, just after this aircraft had been named "Skyliner Whakatane". It was sold on 31 October 1964.
*(Photo: Courtesy Air New Zealand)*

(Below)
Displaying its second QANTAS colour scheme and 'V-JET' logo is short-fuselaged Boeing 707-138B, VH-EBL (c/n 18739) named "City of Geelong". Photographed just prior to delivery in September 1964, this aircraft only served with QANTAS for four years before being sold. It ended up being broken up for spares at Shannon, Ireland. *(Photo Boeing)*

Another classic scene at London-Heathrow Airport in April 1966, with KLM Lockheed Electra PH-LLC passing Channel Airways Hawker Siddeley 748, G-ATEJ (c/n 1587), which had just brought in Sir Peter Masefield, Chairman of the British Airports Authority (note BAA sticker on rear fuselage). This aircraft had only just been delivered when this photograph was taken, yet it was sold the following year. It is still flying, being operated by the Sri Lanka Air Force since 1979.

*(Photo: Bob Griggs)*

(Above)
SABENA operated a fleet of nine Convair 440s during the '50s and '60s throughout Europe, including OO-SCS (c/n 374), which saw service with them from November 1956 to March 1968, when it was sold to Frontier Airlines and converted to a turboprop Cv-580. It is seen during one of its rare idle moments at Heathrow in February 1967.
*(Photo: Brian Stainer)*

(Left)
Depicted at Paris-Le Bourget in 1966, the Ilyushin IL-18 was the Soviet's answer to the Britannia and served with all the Eastern European airlines including Bulgarian Air Transport/TABSO, who operated eleven IL-18s out of Sofia, including LZ-BER. *(Photo: Author's collection)*

A rare sight across the other side of the world at Kai Tak Airport, Hong Kong, on 28 November 1964, with a Douglas DC-3, XW-TAH, of the Laotian airline, Air Vientiane, being towed across the apron. This aircraft's history is unknown, so whether it survives today is a mystery. In the distance can be seen a Japan Air Lines Convair 880, two Douglas DC-4s of Lloyd International and a BOAC Boeing 707.
*(Photo: Bernard B. Deatrick)*

(Above)
A familiar sight at Gatwick throughout the sixties were the Douglas DC-6s of Alitalia's charter subsidiary, SAM-Societa Aerea Mediterranea. DC-6B, I-DIMP (c/n 44417) was leased from Alitalia from December 1961 until it was passed on to the Italian Air Force in 1969. It was finally retired and broken up at Venice in 1975. I-DIMP is seen at Gatwick on 15 August 1968.
*(Photo: Stephen Wolf)*

(Left)
During the sixties, Japan Air Lines domestic fleet included nine Douglas DC-6Bs, including JA6208 (c/n 45067) named "City of Sapporo", seen being towed across the apron at Tokyo-Haneda on 9 October 1967. It was bought from Western Airlines in September 1962 and sold in June 1968. It was last reported in 1981 still flying with the Colombian Air Force.
*(Photo: Bernard B. Deatrick)*

N18667 (c/n 11644) was one of 17 Douglas DC-3s operated by US internal airline, Lake Central Airlines, who started operations in September 1949, based at Indianapolis, and bought this aircraft from Braniff in August 1952. It was withdrawn from use in August 1967 and sold. The following year, the airline was taken over by Allegheny Airlines and subsequently became US Air. This photograph was taken at Chicago-O'Hare Airport on 29 May 1965. (Photo: Bernard B. Deatrick)

(Right) Meanwhile, back at Gatwick in September 1965, Dutch charter airline, Martin's Air Charter had two Douglas DC-7Cs in its fleet of which PH-DSL (c/n 45180) is seen disembarking passengers. Named "Baltic Sea", this aircraft was bought from KLM in November 1964 and sold in December 1968. It was never flown again and remained stored at Stansted until it was broken up in 1981.
(Photo: Werner Gysin-Aegerter)

(Below) Gatwick Airport again, in May 1968, and Channel Airways Vickers V.812 Viscount, G-APPC (c/n 362) is pre-positioned alongside another Viscount of British United Airways. Behind that can be seen a SPANTAX Convair 990A Coronado, a Boeing 727 of Ariana-Afghan Airlines and a VC-10 of British United Airways. This Viscount was one of twelve bought from Continental Airlines, with little change being made to the colour scheme. G-APPC was bought in May 1967, withdrawn from use four months after this photograph was taken and broken up at Southend in June 1972. (Photo: Stephen Wolf)

(Right)
With temperatures slightly lower than what it's used to, IRANAIR Vickers V.782D Viscount, EP-AHC (c/n 299) is seen at Cambridge in 1962 during overhaul by Marshalls. This was one of three Viscounts operated by IRANAIR from May 1958 until it was damaged beyond repair after a heavy landing at Isfahan, Iran, on 15 February 1965. *(Photo: Bob Griggs)*

(Below)
Dublin Airport, Ireland, in August 1968 with Aer Lingus obviously dominating the scene with Vickers V.803 Viscount, EI-AOE (c/n 177) "St Dympna" about to start up, while one of the airline's Boeing 720s can be seen behind. This Viscount was bought from KLM in September 1965 and withdrawn from use in November 1969, being broken up at Dublin in July 1972. *(Photo: Bob Griggs)*

Boeing 707-348C, EI-AMW (c/n 18737) of Aer Lingus named "St Laurence O'Toole" was delivered on 10 June 1964. It was sold to Luxair in June 1972 and last operated by Alyemda, in whose hands it was damaged beyond repair on approach to Damascus, Syria, on 26 January 1982. *(Photo: Boeing)*

(Right)
Air France operated 40 Sud-Aviation Caravelles from 1959 to 1980 on services throughout Europe. Caravelle III, F-BHRE (c/n 9) named "Artois" is illuminated by a shaft of sunlight from an otherwise stormy sky at Paris-Orly in May 1965.
*(Photo: Bob Griggs)*

(Below)
Rarely photographed were the two Vickers V.784 Viscounts operated by Philippine Air Lines, of which PI-C771 (c/n 324) is seen taxying out at Kai Tak Airport, Hong Kong, on 31 August 1965. This aircraft was delivered new to PAL in September 1957 and was sold in April 1967. After use by Skyline of Sweden, it was broken up in October 1971. *(Photo: Bernard B. Deatrick)*

The livery of Scandinavian Airlines System is easily recognisable on this Sud-Aviation Caravelle III, HS-TGG (c/n 49) operated by the newly-formed Thai International assisted by SAS. This was one of four Caravelles leased from SAS, with the front of the cheat line subtly changed from a Viking ship to a Dragon. Previously OY-KRE, it was leased from March 1964 until October 1970. It was then returned to SAS and flew until September 1974 when it was withdrawn from use and broken up in October 1977. The photograph was taken at Kai Tak Airport, Hong Kong, on 13 March 1966. *(Photo: Bernard B. Deatrick)*

Lockheed L-1049G Super Constellation, F-BHBI (c/n 4634) was delivered to Air France in March 1956 and sold in March 1968. One of nine Super Connies operated by Air France, this photograph was taken at Speke Airport, Liverpool, in July 1966 at 1645 hours. This aircraft was withdrawn from use in January 1970 and stored at Arrecife, Canary Islands, but was destroyed by fire in 1984.

*(Photo: via Bob Griggs)*

London Airport, Heathrow, in 1958 with Finnair Convair 440, OH-LRC (c/n 75) being refuelled and a pair of BEA Viscounts in their original colour scheme in the distance. This Convair was one of seven that saw service from 1956 until 1972 with Aero O/Y Finnair. It was last reported in 1984 as being in store at Manila in the Philippines. *(Photo: Bob Griggs)*

(Right)
Although Aeroflot had a vast fleet, their Ilyushin IL-18s were rare visitors to the UK. CCCP-75512 was caught on a foggy day at Heathrow in April 1966 in its original livery. *(Photo: Brian Stainer/APN)*

(Below)
A nice bright winter's day at Munich in December 1965 is all that is required to produce this nice shot of JAT Convair Cv-440, YU-ADK (c/n 461), which was delivered new to the airline in September 1957 until November 1973. It is still flying with Basler Air Service, who bought it in 1986. *(Photo: via Bob Griggs)*

Another Convair 440, this time Danish-registered OY-KPD (c/n 393) "Raven Viking" of Scandinavian Airlines System. This aircraft was delivered new to SAS in January 1957 and sold in September 1970. It was last reported still in service with Trans Continental Airlines on freight duties since April 1985. This photograph was taken in April 1968, but the location is unknown, possibly Copenhagen or Stockholm-Bromma. *(Photo: Author's collection)*

(Above)
A regular sight at London Airport, Heathrow, in 1958, were the Convair Metropolitans of Iberia. Here, Cv-440, EC-AMV (c/n 405) awaits its passengers before departing to a Spanish holiday destination. Iberia was operating seven Metropolitans at the time from 1957 to 1972, when this example was sold to the Spanish Air Force. In 1992 it was still flying in Bolivia. *(Photo: Bob Griggs)*

(Right)
Beautiful Australian weather at Melbourne in 1968 and TAA cargo Douglas DC-3, VH-SBN (c/n 10001) sits with its doors open for the next load of freight. This aircraft joined TAA in September 1946 and was sold in September 1968. It was last known with the Cambodian Air Force. Its current status is unknown.
*(Photo: Author's collection)*

(Left)
Kai Tak Airport, Hong Kong, and Royal Air Lao Douglas DC-4, XW-TAG, which was the sole example of its type operated by this airline at the time, taxies in on 3 November 1965. This aircraft linked Vientiane with Saigon, Bangkok, and Hong Kong until three others joined the airline a few years later. The construction number of XW-TAG is unknown, so its history cannot be related. *(Photo: Bernard B. Deatrick)*

(Below)
Another exotic arrival at Kai Tak, Hong Kong, was the sole Douglas DC-6B, B-1006 (c/n 45550) of Civil Air Transport from Taipei, Formosa. Named "The Mandarin Flight", this aircraft featured a smart colour scheme with buff roof and gold cheat line. It served with the airline for ten years from 1958 to 1968, when it was sold to Royal Air Lao. This aircraft is currently G-SIXC with Air Atlantique at Coventry, who have operated it since March 1987. The photograph was taken at Hong Kong on 4 March 1966. *(Photo: Bernard B. Deatrick)*

(Right)
The typical British weather does nothing to detract from an exotic visitor to Heathrow in April 1966, in the form of Syrian Arab Airlines Douglas DC-4, YK-ADA (c/n 3101). This aircraft was transferred from United Arab Airlines in October 1961. It was damaged beyond repair after overrunning the runway at Damascus, Syria, on 2 October 1966.
(Photo: Brian Stainer)

(Below)
Mascot Airport, Sydney, and Trans Australia Airlines Lockheed Electra, VH-TLA (c/n 1061) arrives after a domestic flight on 4 February 1964. This was one of three Electras operated by TAA from June 1959 to March 1972. It was withdrawn from use and broken up at Seletar, Singapore, in March 1976.
(Photo: Bernard B. Deatrick)

A long way from home is this Douglas DC-7CF, EI-AOC (c/n 45128) of Shannon Air at Kai Tak Airport, Hong Kong, on 31 August 1965. This aircraft was only on lease from March to October 1965, making this photograph rare. This aircraft ended its days when on lease to Airlift International. It crashed on take-off from Tachikawa Air Force Base, Japan, on 12 September 1966. *(Photo: Bernard B. Deatrick)*

Iberia Lockheed L-1049G Super Constellation, EC-AQN (c/n 4645) "La Rabida" on a cargo flight at Heathrow in June 1965. This aircraft was bought from KLM in 1962, converted to a freighter the following year and sold in 1967. It was used on Biafra relief flights and crashed at Port Harcourt, Biafra, in January 1968.
*(Photo: via Dr Jean-M. Magendie)*

(Above)
Yet another Douglas DC-4, this time in Australia. VH-INX (c/n 18327) of Ansett-ANA is actually an ex-USAF C-54B, seen at Essendon, Melbourne, in 1969. This aircraft was also once G-ALEP of Silver City Airways and in service with Ansett-ANA and its predecessors since 1951. It was withdrawn from use in December 1970 and broken up in 1972.
*(Photo: Author's collection)*

(Left)
Seen in its original TAA colour scheme with orange dayglo fin and wingtips is Vickers V.756D Viscount, VH-TVM (c/n 373) "John Fawkner" at Essendon, Melbourne, in November 1959, less than a year after delivery. This Viscount served all its life with TAA, being withdrawn from use and scrapped in May 1970.
*(Photo: via Bernard B. Deatrick)*

A typical dull, wet day at London-Gatwick
Airport on 17 May 1969, one of Donaldson
International Airways' Bristol Britannia
314s, G-APNB (c/n 13426) sits awaiting its
next flight. Named "Carillon", this was one
of a pair of Britannias operated by this
short-lived airline between October 1967
and March 1971. It was scrapped at Luton
in November of the same year.
*(Photo: Stephen Wolf)*

Piston propliner line-up at Basel, Switzerland, in December 1969 with the nearest aircraft being Douglas DC-4 EI-ARS (c/n 27289) of Aer Turas, which was one of the last DC-4s flying in Europe. It was previously HB-ILU of Balair and was about to leave on delivery to Aer Turas, when this photograph was taken. Named "City of Galway", it served with the airline until being sold in April 1977. Since January 1990, this aircraft has been preserved by the USAF and placed on display at Frankfurt, Germany, reverting to its original USAF serial, 44-9063. *(Photo: Werner Gysin-Aegerter)*

(Right)
Another exotic propliner at Kai Tak, Hong Kong, on 31 August 1965 was Royal Air Cambodge Douglas DC-6, F-OCEC (c/n 42878), which was on lease from Air France at the time. It became XU-HAI the following year, then was sold to Air Vietnam in 1969, being withdrawn from use and scrapped in November 1972.
*(Photo: Bernard B. Deatrick)*

(Below)
A familiar sight at Heathrow in May 1964 were the Sud-Aviation Caravelles of Alitalia. Here, Caravelle VIN, I-DABR (c/n 81) "Bellatrix" shows its very smart original colour scheme to advantage, as it taxies by. This aircraft was one of 21 Caravelles that were operated by Alitalia on routes throughout Europe. It was delivered in January 1962, withdrawn from use in October 1975 and broken up.
*(Photo: Bob Griggs)*

A quiet corner of Lydd airfield, Kent, in 1962 with Bristol 170 Freighter Mk.21E, G-AHJI (c/n 12741) "City of Bath" sunning itself resplendent in Silver City Airways colours. This aircraft carried many cars and passengers to France with the airline from December 1955. On 1 January 1963, Silver City was renamed British United Air Ferries and 'HJI continued with them until December 1964, when it was withdrawn from use at Southend and broken up the following year. *(Photo: via Bernard B. Deatrick)*

It is pretty certain that the passengers disembarking this African Safari Airways Bristol Britannia departed in better weather than they arrived in at Gatwick in July 1968. Britannia 313, 5X-UVH (c/n 13431) was one of two used by this airline on safari charters to Kenya, Uganda and Tanzania. It was bought from Globe Air of Switzerland in December 1967 and sold in November 1973. It was withdrawn from use at Stansted in May 1975 and reduced to spares. *(Photo: Author's collection)*

(Left)
Douglas DC-7C, OO-SFC (c/n 45159) was one of nine used by SABENA on international routes until the airline acquired Boeing 707s. In 1961, it was converted to a DC-7CF for cargo duties and it was in that capacity when photographed at JFK Airport, New York, in September 1967. It was sold to SPANTAX in January 1970 and last reported as withdrawn from use in 1979 and stored at Las Palmas, Canary Islands, but has probably since been scrapped. *(Photo: Harry Sievers)*

(Below)
Iraqi Airways was one of the few foreign airlines to order the de Havilland Trident. One of their trio was Trident 1E, YI-AEA (c/n 2125) seen taxying past a Swissair DC-8 at Geneva, Switzerland, on 17 May 1969. This aircraft spent all its life with Iraqi Airways, being delivered in October 1965 and withdrawn from use at Baghdad in June 1977. *(Photo: Author's collection)*

Very rare visitor to London-Heathrow
Airport in 1957 was this Aeroflot Ilyushin
IL-14, CCCP-A1729, with a BEA Viscount
and Ambassador in the background.
*(Photo: Bob Griggs)*

**(Above)**
Globe Air were a Swiss charter airline that operated two Bristol Britannias alongside some Ambassadors and Heralds. Britannia 313, HB-ITB (c/n 13232), was bought from El Al in April 1964 and flew many holiday flights until 20 April 1967, when it was damaged beyond repair after undershooting whilst landing at Nicosia, Cyprus. It was photographed during engine runs at Cambridge in July 1965. *(Photo: Bob Griggs)*

**(Left)**
Sounding just like a Lancaster, Canadair C-4 Argonaut, VR-AAT (c/n) runs up its four Rolls-Royce Merlin engines while serving with Aden Airways in 1961. This was one of three that the airline purchased from BOAC in 1960, whose basic colour scheme they retained. It was sold to Derby Airways in December 1963, who immediately dismantled it for spares use. *(Photo: via Dr Jean-M. Magendie)*

A classic shot of Swissair Convair CV-440 Metropolitan, HB-IMB (c/n 327) at London-Heathrow Airport in 1958 being refuelled and turned round with period vehicles. Named "Fribourg", this was the first of 14 Metropolitans for Swissair, being delivered in June 1956. It was sold to the German Air Force in August 1967. After several other owners, it crashed into Pinarete Mountain, 58 kilometres south of Oaxaca, Mexico, on 21 May 1981. *(Photo: Bob Griggs)*

(Above)
A bright sunny day at Kansas City in October 1967 and Delta Airlines Convair CV-440, N4826C (c/n 391) prepares to depart. This aircraft was delivered new to Delta ten years earlier and sold in March 1970. It was last reported in 1984, still flying in Florida. *(Photo: Harry Sievers)*

(Left)
Yet another Convair 440, N9312 (c/n 426) of Eastern Airlines parked at Miami in 1968. This aircraft was in service with Eastern from May 1957 to June 1970, when it was sold to North East Bolivian Airways who immediately used it for spares at Trinidad, Bolivia. By 1975 it had been broken up. *(Photo: Author's collection)*

With underfuselage pannier, Western Airlines Lockheed L-749A Constellation, N1593V (c/n 2556) is caught during a quiet period at Seattle in October 1968. This aircraft was bought by Pacific Northern Airlines in May 1957, who merged with Western on 1 July 1967. It was withdrawn from use in December 1968, but went on to fly with other operators until 1973, when it was reported abandoned at Lima, Peru and was still there in 1981.

*(Photo: Harry Sievers)*

With its extended wingspan and range, the Lockheed L-1649A Starliner was the definitive variant of the 'Connie' series. Here, N7317C (c/n 1019) TWA's "Star of the Clyde" poses for the camera at San Francisco in 1960. It was delivered to TWA in June 1957, converted to a freighter in November 1960 and withdrawn from use at Honolulu, Hawaii, in December 1968. It was broken up there two years later. *(Photo: Author's collection)*

(Above)
A type featured for the first time in this book is the Martin 4-0-4 of which N40422 (c/n 14128) of Pacific Airlines is seen arriving at San Francisco on 22 September 1966. This aircraft was bought from TWA in September 1960 and sold in June 1968. It was last reported in 1976 with Kodiak Western Alaska Airlines, but its current status is unknown. *(Photo: Bernard B. Deatrick)*

(Right)
You can almost hear the four Pratt & Whitney piston engines thundering overhead, as United Airlines Douglas DC-6, N37538 (c/n 43026) "Mainliner Missouri" is caught on finals to Los Angeles-LAX on 21 March 1965. This aircraft was delivered to United in August 1948 and gave twenty years faithful service with the airline before it was sold. It ended up being scrapped at Fort Lauderdale, Florida, in April 1981.
*(Photo: Bernard B. Deatrick)*

(Left)
Fairchild built 128 F.27 Friendships under licence from Fokker including N2707R (c/n 20) which was delivered to Piedmont Airlines in November 1958, named "Pacemaker James River" and sold back to Fairchild-Hiller in November 1967. It was photographed in January 1967 awaiting its next load of passengers. Air Manila bought the aircraft and operated it until April 1969, when it was withdrawn from use and scrapped at Manila, Philippines.
*(Photo: Author's collection)*

(Below)
The distinctive double-bubble fuselage is readily discernible on Northwest Airlines Boeing B.377 Stratocruiser, N74601 (c/n 15947) named "Stratocruiser Manila" seen at Seattle in the late '50s. Northwest Orient took delivery of this aircraft in July 1949 and after use by Aero Spacelines, it was withdrawn from use at Mojave, California, and scrapped in 1967.
*(Photo: Author's collection)*

Canadair built the Britannia under licence,
gave it a swingtail and re-engined it with
Rolls-Royce Tyne turboprops, resulting in
the CL-44 of which they produced 39 for
civil and military use. CL-44D4-2, N454T
(c/n 24) was delivered to the Flying Tiger
Line in January 1962 for cargo duties. It
was sold to Transmeridian Air Cargo in
December 1969 and last reported in service
with Blue Bell Aviation since August
1981. N454T is seen parked at Bangkok,
Thailand, on 15 June 1969 on a Far East
freight charter flight.
*(Photo: Bernard B. Deatrick)*

Seen arriving at Washington National Airport, DC, in June 1968 is Convair 580, N5835 (c/n 465) of Allegheny Airlines. This aircraft was initially built as a piston-engined Convair 440 for Ansett Airlines and delivered to Australia in October 1957. Allegheny bought it in June 1962 and had it re-engined with Allison turboprops in January 1968. It was sold ten years later and last reported with Air Ontario in 1988. *(Photo: Author's collection)*

These spectators probably didn't realise that this was probably the last time they would see a Pan American Douglas DC-8 at Heathrow, as it comes in to land on 11 August 1968. DC-8-32, N809PA (c/n 45262) named "Clipper Great Republic" served Pan-Am from June 1960 until being sold in October 1968. After several operators, it ended up being broken up at Miami, Florida, in January 1986. *(Photo: Stephen Wolf)*

(Left)
Eastleigh Airport, Southampton, on 25 July 1965 and British United (CI) Airways DC-3, G-ANTC (c/n 26111) sits drying out after a rain shower. This aircraft was bought from Jersey Airlines in August 1963 and operated BUA's Channel Island service until it was sold to Hunting Surveys Ltd, in August 1968. It was last reported in 1983, still flying in Florida.
(Photo: Clive Moggridge)

(Below)
"Flagship Philadelphia", alias American Airlines Lockheed Electra, N6112A (c/n 1051), awaits a new load of passengers at Chicago-O'Hare Airport on 29 May 1965. This was one of 35 Electras that American had delivered in 1959. This aircraft was sold in June 1970 and subsequently flown by several operators before being withdrawn from use at Seletar, Singapore, in December 1987. (Photo: Bernard B. Deatrick)

The landmark in the background is instantly recognisable as the Capitol Building, as Vickers V.745D Viscount, N7440 (c/n 138) taxies in at Washington National Airport in February 1966. This aircraft was one of a batch delivered to Capital Airlines in 1956. On 1 June 1961, they merged with United Airlines and the Viscounts were repainted in the scheme shown here. This and most of United's Viscounts were sold in January 1969, N7440 ending up in Colombia. Its flying days ended when it was damaged beyond repair at Florencia on 14 February 1988.
*(Photo: Author's collection)*

(Above)
Fairchild C-82 Packet, N9701F, was used by Trans World Airlines to transport engines and other spares to stranded TWA airliners around the world. Named "Ontos", it had an auxiliary jet engine on top of the fuselage to assist take-off with heavy loads. It was an occasional visitor to Heathrow during the '50s and '60s, but was photographed at JFK Airport, New York, in May 1967. *(Photo: Harry Sievers)*

(Left)
American Airlines were the largest operators of the Convair 990A Coronado, with N5620 (c/n 30-10-32) being delivered on 21 July 1962. It is seen here at JFK Airport, New York, in July 1967 and was sold to SPANTAX the following January. Two years later, on 5 January 1970, it crashed on take-off at Arlanda, Sweden. *(Photo: Harry Sievers)*

(Right)
North to Alaska and we see the sole Convair 880, N8477H (c/n 22-7-2-54) operated by Alaska Airlines at Anchorage in 1966. Alaska Airlines took delivery of this aircraft in July 1961 and sold it to Cathay Pacific Airways in November 1966. The aircraft was withdrawn from use at Seletar, Singapore, in December 1983 and broken up the following year.
*(Photo: Harry Sievers)*

(Below)
The distinctive gold and black livery is displayed to advantage on Mohawk Airlines Convair 440, N4401 (c/n 483), as it taxies in at Washington National Airport in June 1968. Named "Airchief Black Hawk", it served Mohawk from July 1959 until June 1971 and was still flying in the USA in December 1987. Mohawk were taken over by Allegheny Airlines, who became US Air. *(Photo: Author's collection)*

Selling British airliners to the USA is always a great achievement, no more so than when American Airlines ordered thirty BAC One-Elevens in 1965. This Srs.401AK, N5027 (c/n 67) was delivered on 29 April 1966 and photographed soon after, in July 1966 at Toronto, Canada. It was withdrawn from use in September 1971 and stored until being sold in 1975. It was still flying in 1992, as an executive hack in the USA.
*(Photo: via Dr Jean-M. Magendie)*

**(Right)**
Another US airline to use the BAC One-Eleven was Mohawk Airlines, who took delivery of twenty-three in 1966-67 including Srs.204, N1117J (c/n 99) seen at Washington in December 1966. When Mohawk was merged into Allegheny Airlines on 12 April 1972, this One-Eleven was repainted, then again when the airline became US Air on 28 October 1979. The aircraft was sold in May 1989 and has now been withdrawn from use and stored at Orlando, Florida. *(Photo: Author's collection)*

**(Below)**
Another classic airliner in a classic colour scheme – the Pan American Boeing 707, the symbol of American jet travel in the '60s. This example is a Boeing 707-321, N728PA (c/n 17606) named "Jet Clipper Peerless", seen boarding passengers at Manila, Philippines, on 22 November 1964. This aircraft served Pan-Am from June 1960 until it was sold in June 1971. Coincidentally, it was last used by Air Manila International and was withdrawn from use in October 1982, and placed on display at Manila. *(Photo: Bernard B. Deatrick)*

In a wintery setting, an Eastern Airlines Douglas DC-7 shares a dispersal with one of the airline's Super Constellations. The Douglas DC-7B, N826D (c/n 45335) was delivered new to Eastern Airlines in November 1957 and sold in August 1966. It ended up being broken up in the mid-80s at Paramaribo, Surinam.
*(Photo: Author's collection)*

(Right)
Viewed from the Queen's Building at London Airport, Heathrow, in 1958, Douglas DC-6B, SE-BDR (c/n 43748) "Sture Viking" awaits its passengers. This aircraft was delivered to SAS on 22 February 1953 and sold to the French Air Force in October 1961, but crashed on take-off from Reunion Island on 10 March 1968.
*(Photo: Bob Griggs)*

(Below)
Capital Airlines Vickers V.745D Viscount, N7443 (c/n 199) over Washington DC in 1957. This aircraft was delivered to Capital on 5 October 1956 and passed on to United Airlines when they merged on 1 June 1961. The aircraft was withdrawn from use in February 1968 and broken up at Burbank, California.
*(Photo: Courtesy United Airlines)*

(Above)
One of the identifying features of the Viscount 700 series is the oval forward passenger door, whereas the later 800 series had a rectangular door. This feature is shown to advantage on Vickers V.786D Viscount, G-AVIY (c/n 333) of BKS Air Transport, depicted at Cambridge in March 1968 for servicing by Marshalls. This aircraft was bought from TACA International in May 1967. It was withdrawn from use in April 1970 and broken up at Yeadon. *(Photo: Bob Griggs)*

(Left)
Other regular visitors to Heathrow in the '50s and early '60s were the Douglas DC-6Bs of Swissair. HB-IBE (c/n 43275) was delivered new to Swissair in July 1951 and was sold to Sterling Airways of Denmark in June 1962. Its last flight was on 23 December 1967, when it was damaged beyond repair in a heavy landing at Torslanda-Gothenburg. It is shown basking in the sunshine at London-Heathrow Airport in 1958. *(Photo: Bob Griggs)*

Caledonian Airways were a familiar sight at Gatwick in the '60s and '70s before merging with British United Airways to become British Caledonian and finally being taken over by British Airways. Caledonian's fleet included Bristol Britannia 314, G-ASTF (c/n 13453), which was bought from Canadian Pacific Airlines in January 1966. Seen being repositioned for its next flight at Gatwick in September 1969, the name "County of Perth" can just be discerned on its nose. Caledonian was this Britannia's final operator, being withdrawn from use two months after this photograph was taken. It was scrapped at Gatwick the following year. *(Photo: Bob Griggs)*

The only scheduled operator of the Convair 990 Coronado into Heathrow was Swissair who ordered eight. One of these was HB-ICC (c/n 30-10-12) "St Gallen", which was delivered in January 1962 and was withdrawn from use in March 1975, being donated to the Lucerne Traffic Museum, where it is on display today. HB-ICC was caught between its scheduled services at Heathrow in July 1966.
*(Photo: Brian Stainer)*

(Above)
Long Beach, California, and Western Airlines Lockheed Electra, N7142C (c/n 1128) arrives from a domestic flight on 12 July 1965. Western took delivery of this aircraft from new in May 1961 and operated it for ten years. At the time of going to Press, it was still flying with Zantop International.
*(Photo: Bernard B. Deatrick)*

(Right)
Northwest Airlines Boeing 707-351B, N351US (c/n 18584) seen taxying at Tokyo-Haneda on 5 December 1964. This aircraft was sold to Cathay Pacific Airways in July 1971, who sold in to Lan-Chile in October 1977, in whose hands it crashed on landing at Buenos Aires, Argentina, on 3 August 1978. *(Photo: Bernard B. Deatrick)*

An early customer for the Boeing 727 was National Airlines, who ordered three, the first of which was 727-35, N4610 (c/n 18811) delivered on 23 October 1964. National merged into Pan American World Airways on 7 January 1980 and this aircraft continued in service until being sold in December 1984. It currently flies in military markings with the USAF since October 1985 and is seen here over Washington State in October 1964.
*(Photo: Boeing)*

United Airlines did not operate any Boeing 707s, but was the first airline to put the Boeing 720 into service in 1960, taking delivery of 29. N7203U (c/n 17909) was the third Boeing 720-022 for United, depicted near Seattle just before delivery in April 1960. It spent all its life with United, being withdrawn from use in 1973 and broken up at Minneapolis/St Paul in December 1976. *(Photo: Boeing)*